HAPPINESS HACKS

FOR KIDS

20 ways to help kids realise

their happiness

Richard Bevan & Lisa Bevan

With many thanks and deep gratitude to Myles, Chloe, Maizie, Harry, Pat, Malcolm, Sheila, Mick, Sara, Wayne, Laura, Nicola, Hazel and Rhys.

HAPPINESS HACKS FOR KIDS

20 ways to help kids realise their happiness

Written by Richard Bevan & Lisa Bevan

Edited by Patricia Bevan

POLARITY
PUBLISHING

Polarity Publishing

Dedicated to Seeking Truth and Raising Consciousness

Orders: Please contact Polarity Publishing via the email address: Orders@polaritypublishing.co.uk

ISBN: 978-1-9995810-2-2

First published 2020

Preface

Everybody wants to be happy. It's a Universal truth.

When you ask someone what they desire the most, the vast majority of people will say either "Happiness", "Health" or "Wealth". When pressed further, those who say "Health" or "Wealth" will tell you that they chose "Health" or "Wealth" because they ultimately believe these aspects will enable them to achieve happiness.

So, whilst everybody wants to be happy, we believe that once you become a parent you have an even more overwhelming desire, which is that you want your child to be happy.

The pursuit of happiness is a very intriguing activity. Happiness is an emotional state; therefore, it is possible for any of us to choose to be happy at any given moment, regardless of the circumstances or situations we may be faced with; it's just a choice we have to make.

It is our firm belief that happiness is the natural base state of humanity. If you think about a small infant, it is perfectly happy and contented until it encounters an issue; such as being hungry, cold or having wind. Only then will the infants' emotional state turn from one of happiness to distress, and once the issue is dealt with, they return to being happy.

Likewise, a toddler will be perfectly happy playing with toys or drawing a picture, but this happiness can suddenly end when interrupted by another child taking the toy that is being played with or wanting to share the crayons. Again, once order has been restored, the toddler will go back to being happy and content.

This can also be extended to the toddler being dropped off at nursery, whilst the parent is there, the child may protest, and resist to being left at the nursery. The parent will then leave distressed and be concerned for the rest of the day about their child welfare. When it comes to pick up time, the parent returns with a sense of trepidation about the state of their child. But instead they are greeted with the update that the child was perfectly fine, once the parent had left; the youngster returned to their default state and spent the day happily playing.

We don't believe that this is any different for adults; our natural base state should be one of happiness. Unfortunately, this doesn't seem to be the case for most adults. Based on our own research and observations, it appears that happiness is no longer our natural base state; we have conditioned ourselves to adopt a negative emotion as our base state instead.

So, whilst many of us adults struggle with the notion of choosing to be happy, this in turn will be having an indirect impact on the choices our children make. During the first 0-7 years of a child's life, they are in what's called the imprint stage.

According to the work of **Dr Morris Massy** who is an award winning sociologist, during the imprint stage a child doesn't have the capacity to reason or discern what is occurring around them, as their conscious mind hasn't yet developed, therefore all they can do is soak up, like a sponge, all of the beliefs, behaviours and emotional responses that go on around them and accept it as the truth.

Becoming a parent is probably the most significant change that anyone goes through in life, and no matter how many books you read or videos you have watched or opportunities you have to look after other people's children, nothing every fully prepares you for such a life changing transformation.

Even though becoming a parent is a truly magical and wonderful thing, it can also be one of the most terrifying experiences you can have too.

I remember when my first children were born; it was a two for one deal, as they were twins. I was completely overwhelmed; I had so many apprehensions and fears.

How do I pick them up properly?

Is the content of their nappies meant to be that colour?

Why do they cry when they are tired, surely, they should just fall asleep?

Is there anything in the room that they can harm themselves on?

Am I capable of being a good parent?

The list of questions you ask yourself is just endless and doesn't necessarily put you in the best state of mind to make the choice to be happy and relaxed, and in turn these anxieties can be picked up by your child.

Whilst as a parent our strongest desire is for our child to be happy, the best place to start is with making sure that you are happy. It's exactly the same as the oxygen masks on a plane, make sure you have put your oxygen mask on before helping your child.

The best way to help your child with their happiness is by being a great role model. The unconscious impact you can have as a great role model is immeasurable. Although the hacks outlined in this book are aimed at children, they can actually work just as effectively on adults.

So, whilst we may have a desire to be a great role model for our children, undoubtedly even the best of us will struggle with this from time to time. This is where using some of the hacks in this book can be so valuable, because it proactively guides us down a path of thinking and doing the types of things which will ultimately lead both us and our children to having happier and more fulfilled lives.

Typically, Lisa and I usually work with adults, so this book came about rather accidently. Shortly after writing Happiness Realised – An inside guide to achieving lasting happiness, our younger children's school were looking for a volunteer to come in and talk to the children about aspects of a Growth Mindset.

Growth mindset is a concept which was developed by Psychologist **Carol Dweck** and popularised in her book, *"Mindset: The New Psychology of Success".*

In recent years, many schools and educators have started using Dweck's theories to inform how they teach students, and it was a concept which Lisa and I had conducted trainings on for some teachers from our own local education authority.

Therefore, I volunteered to give a talk at the school for all the students on how happiness can support a growth mindset. The basis of the talk was providing the students with a number of hacks about how they could choose to be happy each day.

The talk was a great success and all of the students were fully engaged and excited by what they had seen. I was soon invited to give the same talk at other local schools.

It was at this point that Lisa and I decided that this notion of happiness hacks could be both useful and valuable to parents, teachers, carers and children everywhere, so we created this short book on what we consider to be some of the most useful hacks for helping children begin to realise and maintain their happiness.

We have broken the book down into five sections, we see these as the main areas where you can support and encourage your child to develop and re-enforce their feelings of happiness. These sections are:

- Gratitude
- Physiology
- Mindfulness
- Self-talk and Questions
- Goals and Intentions

Within each section we then provide a number of hacks. We often use these hacks on our own primary school aged children. These activities were always designed to be fun and engaging, and the results have always been interesting and enlightening.

As you start to use this book yourself with your child, we would encourage you to not treat it as a one-time activity, don't blitz through the book and do all of the hacks in one week. Instead we would encourage you to build the hacks into a regular pattern of activity with your child.

For example, it would be good to get your child to do one or more of the physiologies and mindfulness hacks on a daily basis. Whereas, the hacks in the gratitude and self-talk sections may be something you do less frequently when you are playing with your child.

But ultimately it is up to you and your child as to how you best enjoy and benefit from the hacks in this book. The most important thing is that you start to proactively invest time and energy in cultivating happiness within both yourself and your child.

Visit our websites

www.happinessacademy.online

and

www.polaritypublishing.co.uk

for more information about our trainings, workshops and other books.

Plus, lots of other FREE resources.

CONTENTS

"People are about as happy as they make up their minds to be."

Abraham Lincoln

CHAPTER 1
What is happiness?

CHAPTER 1 - What is happiness?

Before we get into the practical hacks contained in this book, it would be good to have an understanding of how we realise our happiness. So let's first spend some time defining and understanding what happiness is. Each of us will already have our own definition of happiness, but we would like us all to start with a shared common definition.

The dictionary definition of happiness is "the feeling of being happy". This doesn't really tell us too much. So, let's look at the definition of happy, of which there are several different definitions listed below:

- Feeling or showing pleasure or contentment.
- Having a sense of trust and confidence in (a person, arrangement, or situation).
- Satisfied with the quality or standard of......
- Willing to do something.

Let's take each of these definitions in turn and analyse them.

Feeling or showing pleasure and contentment

How often do you or your child display pleasure and contentment? How many times a day do you or your child smile, a real smile, one that comes from your eyes not just your mouth?

How many times a day do you or your child laugh, really laugh, uncontrollably, so much so you temporarily lose the ability to speak.

You and your child need to make time for happiness, no matter what your circumstances are. There will always be some aspect or element of your lives that you can derive pleasure or contentment from: the important thing is providing you and your child with the opportunity to do so.

Having a sense of trust and confidence in (a person, arrangement, or situation)

Let's focus this definition on you and your child.

Do you and your child have a sense of trust and confidence in who you are, and the choices you make?

There is a part of you and a part of your child, often a big part, and other times a meek and mild part, which knows what is right for you. For some, this is the part which will be the nagging or berating voice in your head. For others, it may be the part which gives you a sense of detachment or a sinking feeling.

It's very easy for us all to get wrapped up in what other people think we should be or do. Other peoples' opinions can offer us interesting insights. External recognition, acknowledgements and compliments can be nice, although ultimately, it's self-trust and approval that we need the most. This is particularly relevant to children, because they will often seek approval from their parents or be bombarded with a list of instructions on what they should be doing or thinking.

This doesn't mean that you or your child will always be right or make correct choices, but it does at least mean that you will be listening to yourselves and making your own choices.

It's always difficult for any of us to trust ourselves or have confidence in ourselves if we are not paying attention to ourselves.

Satisfied with the quality or standard of...

Once again, let's focus on this inwardly. Are you and your child satisfied with the quality or circumstances of your worlds?

Let's, for the moment, ignore the superficial things like money and possessions. Let's instead consider the various aspects of our lives, such as:

- Love
- Family
- Friends
- Home
- Health
- Development
- Hobbies

How satisfied are you or your child with each one of these elements? Are you and your child very happy in all these areas, or are you very happy with a few, but very unhappy with some others?

Whilst we all have different lives, hopes and aspirations, and your child's may well be very different to your own. The important thing here is to find a balance and have a positive feeling for each of these elements, rather than one or two that are supercharged.

Willing to do something

Are you and your child willing participants in everything that you currently do?

Are there any activities or tasks which you or your child undertake that are resented, or that you don't believe you should be doing? It's not very often that you or your child will find tasks that you have performed which give you no pleasure or sense of satisfaction. For example, going to school or exercising may not be enjoyable, and the experience may give a feeling of deep displeasure at the time.

However, the satisfaction is felt after the event, with improved fitness or an educated mind. This is all about perception and searching inside yourselves and looking beyond the immediate moment to work out which part of the activity or task you can derive pleasure or satisfaction from.

Are you and your child willing to try something new? For many people routine is a way of managing their fears. There is a time and place for fears; in our estimation, the appropriate time for fear to come into someone's conscious awareness is at the point when we face imminent physical endangerment. This is when fear is designed to initiate the primal response in us to take flight or stay and fight.

Living a fear-based life will definitely have a significant impact on you and your child's ability to realise and maintain a lasting happiness: any fears you have need to be identified, understood and overcome and some of these hacks can assist with that process.

All the elements above which make up the definition of "happy" are things we need to pay regular attention to, and the hacks in this book will help you support your child in doing this. It's very much about making a choice to do these things as a habit. Like anything in life, the more you do something, the better you become at it.

Moving away from the dictionary definition of happiness, let's review a number of other famous definitions of happiness which we believe really illuminate its real essence.

The first example we will look at is from **Mahatma Gandhi**, who was born in Gujarat, India back in 1869. He led India to independence and inspired movements for civil rights and freedom across the world. However, because of his activism he spent many years in prison in both India and South Africa. But despite these potential hardships, he described happiness as:

"Happiness is when what you think, what you say and what you do are in harmony."

Abraham Lincoln also had this insight to share about happiness:

"People are about as happy as they make up their minds to be."

Abraham Lincoln was the 16th President of the United States, taking office in 1861. His words are as true today as they were then. It's all about choice. Like anything else in life, we can determine what it is we want to have and achieve.

Dale Carnegie, the great American author and lecturer, was born into poverty in Missouri, USA in 1888. Whilst in his forties he was responsible for writing several leading self-development books including *"How to win friends and influence people"* and *"How to stop worrying and start living"*. Dale wrote:

"Happiness doesn't depend on any external conditions; it is governed by our mental attitude."

The key message we always take from these words is that the mastery of happiness is completely within one's own control and command, whether you are an adult or a child. There are no dependencies on others, no exams that need to be passed;

it's just a choice, and it's a choice that we need to support our children in understanding and taking.

This knowledge is nothing new. This kind of insightful understanding has been around for thousands of years.

Marcus Aurelius, the (joint) Roman Emperor from 161 – 180 AD, and a practitioner of the Stoicism philosophy, is recorded in his *"Meditation"* notes as saying:

> *"The happiness of your life depends upon the quality of your thoughts."*

If this understanding was grasped so long ago, why do we struggle to put it into practice today?

Our belief is that we are being directed further and further down a consumer-based society, where achievement and obtainment are being used as the measure of happiness.

From the point a child is born, it's likely that they will have to participate in some form of child minding, because frequently today families need to have two incomes to maintain a certain standard of living. The child is then taken into school, the emphasis there is on the obtainment of results, can they read and write as well as their peers? The schools are measured on the standard their students obtain, hence from the age of seven children are being tested to see how they are conforming. Then from midway through senior school, the real pressure to achieve and be measured via external recognition is accelerated. Mock examinations start, ahead of the real examinations a year or so later. These come with a significant societal pressure to get good grades, namely, if you don't get good grades, you won't be able to go to a good University. You need to go to a good University if you want to get a good job. You will need a good job if you want to have a nice car, a nice house, exotic holidays, designer clothes and the latest 4D TV, because if you don't have these things, you'll never be happy.

This philosophy has pushed society to the point where money, wealth and possessions have become the proxy for happiness. We have swapped all these external items, for our own internal and intuitive measure of happiness.

We firmly believe that this is the wrong way around and it's time to redress the balance. We actively support and encourage our children to realise their happiness without any reference to possessions, accomplishment or events.

For us, this was all wonderfully captured by **Frederick Koenig**. Frederick was a German inventor born in 1774 and famous for inventing the high-speed steam-powered printing press, he said:

"We tend to forget that happiness doesn't come as a result of getting something we don't have, but rather of recognising and appreciating what we do have."

The hacks in this book lean heavily on this notion and we will spend time focusing on helping you and your child appreciate what you do have. Happiness is something which is realised, hence the subtitle of this book; and if you are able to support your child in their realisation of happiness it will have a great and profoundly positive impact on their life and your life.

"Anger, hatred and fear are very bad for our health."

Dalai Lama

CHAPTER 2
The Benefits of Happy Kids

Chapter 2 – The benefits of happy kids

Having read chapter 1, we are all now on the same page regarding the definition of what happiness is.

We would also imagine that you intuitively know that living from a happy place for both you and your child is going to provide you all with a better more fulfilled life. Just in case you need a little more persuasion to start trying out some of the hacks in this book, then let us share with you a number of other benefits that are available to children who are happy.

There are 3 main physical health benefits which are fantastic for both adults and children. These are:

1. Happiness helps to reduce stress

Happiness can reduce the levels of stress we experience and help us recover more quickly from situations where we have experienced stress.

Feelings of stress have a measurable impact on both our blood pressure and hormones, studies have shown evidence that both these elements have had a reduced impact in happier people. It appears the happier you are the lower the levels of stress you will experience.

Our children are often put in situations which have the potential to be stressful. For example, they have to go to school five days a week, they are given homework, and they are set tests and exams.

The **Dalai Lama**, spiritual leader of Tibetan Buddhism and the Tibetan people is quoted as saying:

"Anger, hatred and fear are very bad for our health."

It's no surprise to us how this spiritual insight correlates directly to the scientific research which is telling us that happiness seems to be very good for our health. This is born out further by the other elements of this section.

2. Improves general health

Interestingly, research has shown that happiness can have several benefits on our hearts including lowering our heart rate (i.e. the time between our heart beats) and reducing our blood pressure. This has been demonstrated to lower the risk of cardiovascular disease in later life.

Researchers have also explored how people with different degrees of happiness respond to being exposed to different diseases and illnesses; these have included the common cold and the hepatitis B vaccine. Evidence has been gathered to demonstrate that the happier individuals were able to generate a greater number of antibodies to counteract the illnesses they were being exposed to, which is a measurable sign of a stronger immune system.

Schools are usually where your child will be exposed to a whole host of potential diseases and illness, so having them be happy is e a great way of reducing this risk.

3. Nature's painkillers

Have you ever noticed how unhappy people seem to suffer from aches, pains and other conditions? We often wonder which came first the unhappiness or the aches and pains. Positive emotions and feelings of happiness have the ability to lessen the feelings of constant pain. This is primarily due to the increased levels of endorphins that are produced in the bloodstream, effectively becoming nature's own painkillers.

Maybe this is something to be considered next time you are reaching for the medicine cabinet for your child.

In addition to the physical health benefits there are also a number of less tangible benefits, which are fantastic for adults, but if you think about children going through such a huge amount of social and academic development then these benefits are amazing.

1. Broader focus

When you are happy you can expand your focus of attention to be across a broad array of things. You will not just be focused on one thing, which is often how we are when we are experiencing a negative emotion, such as frustration, despair or anger.

During the negative emotion your focus narrows to the cause of your negative emotion. You will struggle to put aside the thing that is bothering you.

My personal experience has been when something has got me particularly frustrated, I become singularly focused on resolving my point of frustration, and for a period, nothing else matters. Whereas, when I'm happy and excited, I experience the opposite, I find that my perceptions and awareness start to expand; I begin to flow with what I'm doing, and I can be far more creative.

2. Improved learning State

When we are happy our ability to learn and absorb information is increased. The most effective teachers are typically those who can put the students at ease and make the process of learning fun.

When doing my own distance learning Open University studies, I would always find that if I had a good day at work, I would be able to read my study books with ease. If I'd had a bad day and was still dwelling on some aspect that had annoyed me, nothing would go in. I could read the same passage several times and absolutely nothing would stick.

When we are children, this is the period where we are exposed to most of our learning opportunities. So, an improved learning state will definitely be of benefit to your child.

3. Increase social interaction

Oscar Wilde, the renowned poet and playwright, born in Dublin in 1854 is said to have quipped:

> *"Some people cause happiness wherever they go, others whenever they go."*

I find this statement both insightful and relevant to us today, when somebody walks into a room; it is usually obvious to you what mood they are in before they have even said a word. Unconsciously you will be able to judge their state based on a combination of their facial expressions and mannerisms. It's also possible to judge this via the energy that they are giving off. If you sense the person is angry, annoyed or depressed, you may attempt to avoid them or reduce the length of time you are interacting with them.

When your child is happy, their happiness will radiate from them to everyone around. This will be attractive to others and they are far more likely to have people wanting to interact with them, and because they are happy, they will want to engage with that interaction too.

So enough of the setup and justification; let's now start going through the HAPPY HACKS FOR KIDS (and adults).

"Gratitude is the magnifying glass of life. Everything seems to be bigger, better and brighter when viewed through the lens of gratitude."

Richard Bevan

CHAPTER 3
Gratitude

Chapter 3 – Gratitude

Gratitude is the magnifying glass of life. As you look through the lens of gratitude everything will seem bigger, better and easier to comprehend. Doesn't the land of gratitude sound like a wonderful place for you and your child to live in?

You see, gratitude has very similar qualities to happiness; it is a free resource that is self-generated and self-perpetuating. Once you and your child begin to head down the path of gratitude, you will be able to reach any destination in life and it's a major contributor to you and your child being able to realise happiness.

To give it some context, gratitude is just a strong feeling of appreciation to someone or something, for what has been gifted to you. In today's modern society it becomes increasingly easy for us all to lose sight of many things that are easily and instantly available to us, for which we could and probably should feel a great sense of gratitude.

As adults we are often trapped into thinking about the next tasks or activity that will consume us, without taking a moment to stop and think about what we already have, or what has just happened to us. This is increasingly the same for our children; there are constant pressures to achieve something new or live up to the expectations of their peer groups. The time for play and reflections has been severely diminished.

There has been an increasing amount of research into establishing the benefits of gratitude, the research has shown that gratitude in adults has physical, psychological, and social benefits. This has included increasing both happiness and well-being, lowering blood pressure, improving the immune function and decreasing feelings of loneliness and isolation.

If these benefits have been established for adults there is every reason to believe children will receive the same benefits, in particular the increasing of happiness and well-being, which is why we have included a gratitude section in this book.

If you consider your normal day, there are so many things that you could choose to feel gratitude towards.

When you woke up this morning, were you grateful that you had a warm dry bed to sleep in? Or, did you think about how you wish you had a bigger bedroom or maybe you wished your alarm clock wasn't going off so early.

When you had your shower and brushed your teeth were you grateful that you had access to running water directly into your house? Or do you just take it for granted and pay it no attention.

It may be that you and your children do already express thankfulness or gratitude, saying thank you for certain things. But the key to true gratitude is not just the saying of words out of politeness or etiquette.

True gratitude is like a spiritual connection between you and the other person, a connection and an energy exchange that both parties will feel and absorb the benefit of.

If you truly appreciate something, it will radiate and vibrate from within you and others will want to bring more of it to you. They do this because they will also gain benefit from having willingly given something that is greatly valued and appreciated by someone else.

Gratitude will make you and your child feel good and in turn this will lead to doing good things for others. When you are the recipient of an act of kindness or generosity, it can motivate you to do the same for others in the future.

Gratitude is a social emotion; fostering this in yourself and your child can lead to benefits for all our greater good. Actively participating in gratitude will help your child nurture and strengthen relationships, appreciate they are part of something greater than themselves and act as an emotional buffer during any tricky times. The more we can help our children bolster their resilience, the happier they will become.

If you and your child are able to be grateful for what you already have, this will fuel your unconscious mind to be on the look out to bring you more of the things that you are already grateful for.

The more you are in a state of gratitude, the more you will attract things to be grateful for; if you focus on what you don't have, then you'll never have enough. But the key here is having a true and unequivocal emotional response of gratitude, and not just creating a list of things that you could be grateful for in the hope of gaining more.

Being happy won't always lead to you being grateful, but feeling and expressing gratefulness, will always make you happy. It's impossible to sincerely appreciate a moment and be unhappy about it at the same time. To be happy right now doesn't mean that you have everything you want and don't have a desire for more; it means you're grateful for what you already have and are ready to be patient for what's yet to come.

So, if you and your child are able to pause on a daily basis to give thought and thanks for the things that you are grateful for, it will not only make you and your child feel good, it will also accelerate the realisation of happiness.

HACK
1
THANKFULNESS THEMES

The hack below is aimed at your child, but it could work equally well for yourself. Or even better, it could be one that you can do together.

The idea of this hack is to give your children a way in which they can easily think of things that they enjoy and are thankful for. Being thankful for something is the first step on the path to having a sense of gratitude. So, this is a great way to introduce your child to the concept of gratitude.

Hack Time – 10mins

What you will need – A sheet of paper, a pencil, egg timer or stopwatch.

How it works

Start by creating a list of 10 categories of things that you could be thankful for, below is an example list.

1. Activities
2. Animals
3. Books
4. Films
5. Foods
6. Friends
7. Grown-ups
8. Places
9. Songs
10. Toys and Games

Keep the list out of the view of your child and ask your child to pick a number between 1 and 10.

Then for the category they have selected by choosing the number between 1 and 10, give them 1 minute to write down or say aloud for you to write down, all of the things they are thankful for within that particular category.

We would recommend only doing 3 categories in each session.

Once you have the list of the items for the selected category, ask your child to review the list and select the one that they are most thankful for.

So, let's imagine your child has completed the exercise for Toys and Games, and the item they are most thankful for is their Harry Potter Top Trump cards.

Then you need to ask your child to close their eyes and spend 30 seconds thinking about why they are so thankful for their Harry Potter Top Trump cards, at the end of the 30 seconds ask your child to give you three reasons why they are thankful for the cards.

Just make a note of the three reasons, there is no need to comment or make a judgement on their reasons.

The purpose of this exercise is to get your child into a joyous, thankful and happy state.

Repeat the Hack on different days, letting your child select different category numbers each day.

HACK
2
COMPETITIVE BLESSINGS

This is a great hack for both you and your child to participate in.

The purpose of this hack is to come up with a list of all the things that you and your child have been blessed with that day. This could consist of anything that you or your child considers to be a blessing. It could be small blessings, large blessings, obscure blessings, practical blessings, blessings which you have received directly, or blessings which you have given to others.

The size and shape of each blessing is irrelevant, the most important aspect is that every single one of them is a blessing.

This is basically just a numbers game. If your child is able to point to a large number of blessings it can provide a much-needed emotional boost when something bad has come their way.

Counting blessings is a sure way to develop a constant mind-set of gratitude, which can turn a mundane life into a miraculous one. I see this as almost counting your way to the realisation of happiness.

Hack Time – 10mins

What you will need – A sheet of paper, a pencil.

How it works

Start by deciding how many blessings you want to capture on your list that day. I would suggest a number between 20-50 would be a good number.

A list could look something like this.

Blessing 1 – Frosties for breakfast

Blessing 2 – A lift to school

Blessing 3 – No homework

Blessing 4 – Playing football at lunchtime

Blessing 5 – Learning something new

Blessing 6 – The sun was shining

Blessing 7 – A friend saved them a seat

Blessing 8 – The uniform was warm from the tumble dryer

Blessing 9 – Being given a new school reading book

Blessing 10 –Their water bottle was full of fresh water

Blessing 11..

Then you and your child should spend up to 5 minutes trying to get to the prescribed number of blessings you are targeting.

The winner is the person who reaches the target number first. However, if you are not able to reach the target number in the 5 minutes allocated, then the winner is the person who came up with the most blessings.

The winner then gets to read out their list to the other person.

Again, there is no need to comment or make a judgement on your child's list of blessings. The important element of this hack is that they are taking the time to identify and appreciate that they have a significant number of blessings.

HACK
3
WHAT IF IT WERE GONE

This is a hack which you can use to get your child to gain an understanding, appreciation and a gratitude for items that most of us in the western society take for granted.

It's good for children to understand that many of the items that we are blessed with in the western world haven't always been so readily available and accessible, and the fact that they have them in their life is both a source of convenience and happiness.

Hack Time – 10mins

What you will need – N/A

How it works

Use the example list of items below, take one item at a time and ask your child to think about what life would be like if they didn't have them.

Example list:

1. Drinking water
2. A bed to sleep in
3. Laughter
4. The Internet
5. Food in the fridge
6. Trees
7. Clothes
8. The sun
9. The rain
10. Favourite toy

Ask your child to imagine the world without an item listed above, for this example, let's use "trees".

Then run through the following list of questions.

Question 1 – What would it be like to not have "trees"?

Question 2 – How many times a day are they affected by or interact with "trees"?

Question 3 – Would their life be easier or harder without "trees"?

Question 4 – What would having no "trees" stop them from doing or having?

Question 5 – If "trees" didn't exist what would they need to have instead?

Question 6 – What could replace "trees"?

Question 7 – Who else would be affected if "trees" didn't exist?

Question 8 – Are there any things that they would give up to ensure they always had "trees"?

To make the hack more fun, you could ask your child to come up with a list of items for you to play the "what if were gone" game with.

When you have gone through all 10 of the examples above, you can create your own additional list of items. I would avoid using specific named people on any of your lists, as the thought of somebody not being there, could be quite distressing for your child.

HACK
4
SCAVENGER HUNT

This is a hack which you can use to get your child actively and physically engaged in items they are thankful or grateful for.

It's a great way to indirectly promote the message of gratitude whilst fully participating in a regular playtime activity.

This is a great hack, the combination of movement, e.g. looking for the items and thinking about things that they are thankful or grateful for, pushes on two of the doors which lead to happiness.

Hack Time – 20mins

What you will need – A sheet of paper, and a pencil.

How it works

Start by creating a list of about 10 items which your child can find around your house or garden that they are thankful for.

An example list would look like this:

1. Find something that makes you happy

2. Find something that is useful to them

3. Find something that you love which someone gave you

4. Find something that you can give to someone else

5. Find something that you love in nature

6. Find something you love the feel of

7. Find something you love the look of

8. Find something you love the sound of

9. Find something you love the taste of

10. Find something you love the smell of

Share the list with your child and give them 10-15 minutes to find one example of each of the items on the list.

When the time is up, ask your child to show you each of the items and tell you why they selected it.

Again, there is no need to comment or make a judgement on your child's list of selected items or their reasons for selecting the items.

This also works well the other way round, you could ask your child to compile a list for you to do a scavenger hunt with, at the end of the activity when you have gathered all of the objects you can ask your child to say why they think you selected each item.

"All human movement is expressive."

Alexandra Pierce

CHAPTER 4
Physiology

CHAPTER 4 – Physiology

Physiology is all about the functions and movements of the body.

This includes all of the body organs and bodily functions, how we are standing, e.g. upright or slouched and our facial expressions, e.g. smiling or frowning.

This notion of physiology is key to happiness hacks because by consciously modifying our physiology we can have both dramatic and instant control over how we feel.

Completely unconsciously you and your child will determine your emotions and subsequent actions by the following process.

External events outside of you or your child will be absorbed through your five senses

- Eyes
- Ears
- Touch
- Smell
- Taste

There are so many external bits of information that can be absorbed and observed through the five senses, it is estimated that approximately 20 million bits of information per second are available to us; this information has to be filtered by the unconscious mind.

This filtering is undertaken by the unconscious mind through the following processes

- Deletion
- Distortion
- Generalisation

Deletion of the information is literally as it suggests, certain parts of the available information are deleted or dismissed which then dramatically reduces the information being received. We therefore quite literally focus on what we think is important, despite the actual reality.

Distortion is when we unconsciously exaggerate or intentionally corrupt the information being received to make it is easier for the information to be taken onboard. This can often lead to people over re-acting to something.

Generalisation is when the information being received is deliberately adapted and pigeon-holed to fit an understanding or belief we already hold.

Once the information has gone through the filtering process outlined above, it is then reduced to between 5-9 chunks of information; this is all the mind can handle without being totally overwhelmed. These 5-9 chunks of information are what the mind uses to generate its internal representation of what has occurred. This representation is not the actual event, but instead, it is a version of the event which has been calibrated against all of the existing beliefs, values and decisions already held by you or your child.

So, this internal representation really is just a version of the reality. This process is one of the reasons why two people will rarely have the same interpretation when both witnessing a specific event.

From this internal representation, you and your child will then determine your state. Your state is just your way of being or your mood.

The derived state then manifests itself in you and your child's physiology, for example, if the state was sadness or upset, the body will slump, the shoulders will droop, the eyes will be looking downward, and the mouth will drop down at the corners. The bodies' physiology will generally be soft and floppy. By contrast if one was in a happy state, the body would be straight and erect, with the head up and the mouth would be smiling. The chest would be puffed up and the shoulders would be pinned back.

Then the final part of the process is that a combination of the state and physiology that is being adopted by you or your child will then determine any subsequent behaviours and outcomes.

As you can imagine if your child's state is not a positive one, then their subsequent behaviours are likely to be muted or limited. Whereas, if your child's state was a very positive one, then their subsequent behaviours are likely to be much more intense and creative.

The great thing about the unconscious process described above is that there is an opportunity to manipulate and control part of the process; your child's state (i.e. mood) will derive their physiology. This also works equally well the other way around; your child can change their state by consciously adopting a different physiology.

Therefore, if you are able to help your child become aware of their state, then there will always be an opportunity to override the state and select a more useful and resourceful state, just by purposefully adopting the relevant physiology of the desired state.

The eminent psychologist **Robert Plutchik** (21 October 1927 – 29 April 2006) who was at the Albert Einstein College of Medicine created the *"Psycho evolutionary"* theory of emotion; he identified eight primary emotions, listed below.

- Anger
- Sadness
- Fear

- Joy
- Anticipation
- Surprise
- Disgust
- Shame

Each one of the emotions listed above will have its very own specific physiological responses. As **Alexandra Pierce**, the composer, music theorist and movement educator said:

"All human movement is expressive."

There is therefore a huge amount of power in your child understanding and being able to recreate and adopt these physiological effects for any of the positive emotions; this can have a rapid and beneficial impact on your child's ability to realise their happiness.

HACK
5
HAPPY STANCE

This hack is all about providing your child with a shortcut to feeling happy by taking on the physiology of someone in a happy state.

The key physiological features and attributes of someone in a happy and joyous state are the following:

- Standing upright
- Shoulders back
- Smiling
- Chin up
- Chest forward

Just by adopting these characteristics your child's state will instantly change, which in turn will impact their subsequent behaviours and outcomes.

Hack Time – 2mins

What you will need – N/A

How it works

When you notice your child is not in a positive, happy and resourceful state ask them to do the following:

- Stand up

- Stretch their back out so it's as straight as possible

- Raise their chin so it is about 3cm's above the horizontal

- Put their arms down by their side and pull their shoulders back so their chest puffs forward

- Smile so much that their teeth are showing

Once your child has adopted the happy stance outlined above, have them hold this pose for 10 seconds.

After 10 seconds, ask your child to continue to hold the pose and this time get them to shout YES, YES, YES repeatedly either aloud or in their heads for a further 10 seconds.

After this your child will have adopted a happy state due to their physiology and will be able to be much more productive and creative.

You can check if your child has adopted a happier state, immediately after the hack is complete ask them to describe their mood.

If you don't get an indication that your child is now feeling in a more positive state, then you can repeat the exercise above. However, due to the mind body connection it is almost impossible to feel negative emotions while you are adopting the characteristics of a positive physiology.

This exercise works equally well for adults, I would recommend that it is something worth doing every time you notice your own state is not in a good place.

Don't forget that acting as a role model for your child is equally as good as doing the hacks with them.

HACK
6
WALK AND TALK

This hack is all about using the natural flow of human energy during moderate movement, and association with nature, to help your child to communicate and share any issues that are causing them to feel uptight and unhappy.

Energy should be able to freely flow around your child's body, often a lack of physical movement combined with negative emotions can cause the energy to become blocked and stifled. Therefore, engaging in physical activity can have a positive and quick effect on helping your child's energy to begin to flow again.

This hack can act as both a distraction tactic for your child and a stimulant for moving blocked energies. These two factors help with releasing transitory negative emotions or at least act as the trigger for them to be vocalised.

The method of walking and talking is becoming an increasingly popular format used by both coaches and therapists. It is often combined with interacting with nature; the influences of nature can be very relaxing and help your child gain a better context and perspective to frame whatever their current issue may be.

Hack Time – 20mins

What you will need – Access to the outside, ideally somewhere with grass or greenery.

How it works

If you notice your child looks unhappy or upset and is not willing to share with you what has upset them, then undertake the following hack.

Invite your child to come outside and have a walk with you. If possible and safe to do so, walking with bare feet on a surface like grass or sand can enhance the results of this hack.

Walk together for about 5 minutes, and then begin introducing elements of nature into your conversation. You can do this by asking them to do some of the following activities:

- Look up at the top of a tree
- Smell a flower
- Feel the surface of a leaf or the bark of a tree
- Listen for different types of bird song
- What does the ground feel like on their feet (If your child is bare foot)

During the next five minutes you can then ask the child the following types of questions:

- What has been there favourite part of the day so far?
- What are the things which have gone well today?
- Is there anything which could have gone better today?
- Are there any other things which they would like to share?
- Do they have anything which they would like to start again with today?
- Is there anything they want to forgive themselves or others for?
- Is there anything that is troubling them today?

Sometimes it can also be helpful to ask yourself these questions first and share your answers with your child to help open up the conversation.

Sometimes just the act of walking can change your child's state from upset back to being happy.

But if your child does have something they want to share with you. Once you have understood the issue, then you can reassure your child that everything is okay.

Finish off by offering up ways in which they can have a more positive perspective by using some of the hacks in the self-talk and questions section of this book.

HACK
7
MEGA VISION

This hack is all about helping your child get into a relaxed state; it works very well for reducing anxiety and helping your child get into a state that will enable them to engage the creative part of their brain.

When a person focuses their vision on something specific e.g. reading a book, it's called foveal vision. You can only really see the thing you are concentrating on. Everything in the periphery looks a little fuzzy, some say it's a little bit like looking through a tube. Can you imagine being in foveal vision all day. It can make you start to feel stressed and uptight.

The other way of seeing things is called peripheral vision. This is where you get to see a lot more. It enables you to see everything around you clearly, whilst still having the ability to put your focus on a specific object.

Being able to get into peripheral vision, or mega vision as we prefer to call it, will help your child stay concentrated for longer periods whilst maintaining a calm persona.

By removing any nervousness your child has, it will help them to think more happily, constructively and positively.

Hack Time – 5 mins

What you will need – A spot on the wall.

How it works

Ask your child to come and sit down and get them to pick a spot on the wall that they can look at comfortably. You may want to put a spot on the wall before starting the hack.

The spot should be above their eye line and directly in front of them.

Ask your child to keep focussing on that spot for about 10 seconds. Remind them that it's okay to blink whilst they focus on the spot.

Then ask your child to slightly extend their field of vision, so that you are looking at the spot and about 30cm either side.

After a further 15 seconds ask your child to slowly take their vision out a little more until they can't focus on the spot anymore; they will start to see any objects either side of them. Ask your child to tell you what they can see, this will help you determine if they are in mega vision.

If your child is struggling to expand their vision, get them to loosen their jaw, take a few deep breaths and go back to the previous step and start again.

Ask your child to stretch their vision even wider and then attempt to stretch their awareness of their imagination to cover as far around them as possible.

This is the point where your child will be in mega vision (peripheral vision) and then ask them to do their best to remain in mega vision for the remainder of the day. This may take some practice and if they find themselves coming out of mega vision during the day, they could just take a quiet moment to re-do the activity.

Mega vision (peripheral vision) is also known as the learning state. So, this is a great hack to have your child do on a daily basis, prior to going to school. Reminding your child to use mega vision throughout the day, will greatly enhance your child's ability to take in and retain information during the school day.

HACK
8
SUPER BREATHS

Very similar to Hack 5 (Happy Stance), this hack also provides a quick way to alter your child's state and levels of both relaxation and awareness. This time instead of using the body's physiology, your child should focus on altering their breathing technique to gain a similar affect.

Our unconscious minds breathes for us effortlessly in excess of 20,000 times a day. Begin to imagine the impact that your child can have by taking conscious control of their breathing for a short period of time each day, with the specific intention of increasing their happiness and wellbeing.

The Super Breaths hack gives you and your child a very simple technique that will let you take conscious control of your breathing, which will result in increased energy, a more alert state, and it will also quieten a busy mind whilst providing a sense of real calmness.

Hack Time – 5 mins

What you will need – N/A

How it works

1. Ask your child to come and sit with you. We would suggest you either sit on the floor with your legs folded under you or alternatively you could sit on the edge of a chair with legs positioned slightly in front.

2. Ask your child to bring their arms up to their side, bent at the elbow with your hands in loose fists next to the shoulders.

3. They are now ready to start the Super Breaths.

4. Ask your child to begin with a deep breath in, then out.

5. Then ask your child to take in a quick full breath through their nose, whilst simultaneously raising their arms straight up all the way above their head and open their palms.

6. Then immediately breathe out through their nose and at the same time rapidly bring their arms back into the original position by their sides, back into fists.

Repeat steps 4, 5 and 6 at a steady pace making 15 – 20 breaths. Then relax for 30 seconds.

Then repeat steps 4, 5 and 6 again at a steady pace for a further 15 – 20 breaths. Remember that your child should only breathe in and out through their nose.

We would recommend that both you and your child introduce the Super Breath hack into your daily morning routine; it is a great way to feel invigorated, happy and alert for the rest of the day.

"Mindfulness means being awake. It means knowing what you are doing."

Jon Kabat-Zinn

CHAPTER 5
Mindfulness

CHAPTER 5 – Mindfulness

Mindfulness is a term that we hear everywhere nowadays, and this is for good reason; being mindful is a simple method that allows us to connect the two sides of our mind, our conscious mind and our unconscious mind.

Mindfulness is about being able to pay full attention to something. It is when we use our ability to really slow something down enabling us to fully notice what it is that we are doing.

Being deliberately mindful is very effective for adults; we live in a world where we seem to be racing around at 1000 miles per hour, constantly feeling pressured to rush tasks and always having to multitask. How often do you really give yourself the opportunity to focus on just one task in a calm and relaxed way?

An increasing amount of scientific research, and our own intuitions, will tell us that mindfulness is undoubtably good for us. Particularly as parents, it enables us to be present in our parenting, choosing skilful responses to situations and questions, instead of just succumbing to frustrated emotional responses.

Unfortunately, our children are beginning to be subjected to very similar pressures as we as adults do. They too have many conflicting pressures and priorities. Along with increasing amounts of schoolwork and tests, they also have the pressures of managing friendships and classroom dynamics, which now extent beyond the school day, as social media proliferates our children's worlds at an increasingly younger age.

Mindfulness is therefore also extremely beneficial for your child. There is an emerging body of research that indicates mindfulness can help children improve in a number of different areas including:

- Paying attention
- Remaining calm under pressure
- Not becoming upset irrationally
- Increasing concentration
- Increasing the ability to learn
- Being methodical and not rushed
- Remaining in control
- Increasing cognitive abilities
- Being able to listen to information better
- Being more patient
- Building more meaningful friendships

And most important of all
- Feel happier
- Enjoy a better sense of fulfilment

So, as we can see from the list above, there are a huge amount of benefits to teaching our children mindfulness as it will give them the necessary skills to develop both awareness of their inner thoughts and their subsequent outer experiences.

Along with other sections in this book, supporting your child in developing mindfulness, will give them a better grasp on how their emotions arise and how they can be controlled. It also provides them with a mechanism for purposefully choosing when and what they really want to focus their attention on.

As we have mentioned a couple of times in this book, the best way to teach your child is to be a good role model and mindfulness is no different. We would highly recommend that you establish your own daily mindfulness practices, as this will provide you with the best platform to share these hacks with your child.

Mindfulness is not as complicated as it sounds, and it's very likely you are already participating in several mindfulness related activities on a daily basis. Examples could be:

- Focusing on what your child is saying when they are telling you about their day
- Enjoying your daily shower or bath
- Finding 15 minutes a couple of times a week to go running
- Enjoying some peace and quiet on your daily commute

If you can also add a daily 10-minute meditation into this list too, then you will really be flying.

The American Professor and Buddhist **Jon Kabat-Zinn** sums up mindfulness very well with his quote:

"Mindfulness means being awake. It means knowing what you are doing."

Playing sport is probably the best way which most people experience a deep sense of mindfulness. If you are in the middle of a tennis rally or about to take a shot at goal in a football match, then it's impossible not to be mindful; you will be totally focused on the pursuit of your particular sporting activity. The same can be said for singing or dancing too, these activities demand that you focus on them and it becomes a very pure form of mindfulness.

As we undertake the hacks outlined over the next few pages it is important that we don't over complicate what mindfulness is. Essentially all you want to do is help your child understand that mindfulness is just awareness. It's about your child noticing their thoughts, feelings, body and anything that is going on around them in a specific given moment.

They are essentially just paying full attention to something. It's not a superpower or special skill, but it is a skill that both adults and children have become very disconnected with because there are just so many external sources of information and interruptions that occur on such a frequent basis. Social media messages, text messages, TV adverts, other people's opinions, etc.

Being mindful helps people in almost every part of life. Learning how to be mindful when you are young gives you a chance to get really good at it and use it all the time. Like most things in life, your child will need to practice mindfulness to become accomplished at it. Consequently, we would strongly recommend that you and your child incorporate at least one of the hacks in this session into your daily routine.

HACK
9
DESCRIBABLE ME

This hack is a great way to get your child to become aware of how they are feeling throughout their body and mind.

The Describable Me hack gives your child an easy technique to be mindful, without having to engage in understanding what mindfulness is, it enables them to go inside themselves and become aware of what they are thinking and feeling in different parts of their body.

We don't often give the individual parts of our body enough focus and attention, so this is a great way to be aware and thankful for all the parts of our body.

Hack Time – 10 mins

What you will need – Relaxing background music.

How it works

Start by playing some gentle relaxing instrumental music.

Ask your child to come and sit down on a chair where their feet can touch the ground without their shoes on.

Then ask your child to put their hands in their lap and close their eyes and relax for 30 seconds.

Then after 30 seconds, ask your child to focus on their feet and describe how their feet feel against the floor. What feelings do they have in their feet?

Then ask your child to move their attention up to their knees and ask them to describe what feelings they have in their knees. If your child can't come up with anything, then maybe make suggestions, do they feel warm, itchy, cold, aching or flexible?

After your child has explored the feelings in their knees, ask them to move their attention to the feelings they get from being sat on the chair.

Then, ask your child to move their attention up towards their torso, and ask them to describe what feelings they have in their tummy and their chest.

You can also ask them to describe any feeling which they have in their heart. You can focus on asking them whether they can feel their heartbeat, is it fast or slow, regular or irregular, strong or weak.

Ask your child to then focus on their neck and their throat, ask them to share with you what feelings they have in their neck and throat. Ask if there is anything else that they want to say.

Next ask your child to start describing what they can see with their eyes closed, are there any colours or shapes which they can see behind their eye lids.

Finally ask your child to move their attention to the top of their head. What are they thinking, are they able to describe what they are feeling?

At the end of the hack bring your child gently back into themselves by asking them to open their eyes on the count of 5.

You may find your child isn't able to stay focused for the whole hack for the first few times. This is fine, just keep them going for as long as they remain interested.

HACK
10
MINDFUL MUNCH

This is a great hack you can do with your child at any mealtime. The objective is to get your child focused on what it is that they are consuming into their body.

In a world of convenience food, takeaway's and TV dinners, this hack provides you and your child with an opportunity to have a calm, focused, reflective and mindful meal together.

This hack can work particularly well when you have a group of children, because it doesn't only get the children mindful about what they are eating, they also have to be mindful about listening to other people's thoughts and views.

Hack Time – 20 mins

What you will need – Breakfast, lunch or dinner.

How it works

Prepare breakfast, lunch or dinner, any meal or snack will do.

Sit down with your child and ask them which bit of the food they would like to try first.

When they have selected the item of food they want to start with, ask your child to describe to you the following things:

- How does the food look?
- How does the food smell?
- What is the texture of the food like?
- How does the food feel in their mouth?
- How does the food taste?
- What do they think the food will do for their body?

To give your child the maximum chance of really experiencing and appreciating the food that they are eating, it's very important that they attempt to eat in a very slow and deliberate manner.

Once your child has described all of the above to you, then you should try the same bit of food and describe all of the above to your child. Or if you are eating with multiple children, each child should be given a chance to describe their answers to all the above questions.

Then move on and ask your child to select the second bit of food they would like to try and run through the same list of questions again.

Again, you should then try the same bit of food and describe your answers to the questions.

Repeat this pattern until both you and your child have finished your meals.

It may be difficult to get your child to stay focused throughout the course of a whole meal; it may be better to get them to stay focused for the first bite of each of the different foods available to them.

HACK
11
SAILBOAT BREATHING

One of the best ways for your child to enjoy the benefits of being mindful and realising happiness is to train themselves to be able to just focus their attention on one thing at a time.

This hack is a great way to help your child to develop that skill in a very calm and relaxed way.

Hack Time – 5 mins

What you will need – N/A

How it works

Start by playing some gentle relaxing instrumental music.

Ask your child to come and sit down with you in a relaxed, comfortable position.

Then ask your child to close their eyes and just focus on their breathing. Gently breathing in through their nose and out through their mouth.

Ask them to imagine when they are breathing in that they are sucking in oxygen like they are a mini vacuum cleaner. And when they are breathing out ask your child to imagine they are blowing a sailboat along with the air they are exhaling.

Their job is to be able to suck in enough air so they can blow the imaginary boat all the way back to shore.

To help them stay focused, and to assist you with observing that they are focused, ask your child to hold their arms wide apart and bring them together slowly as the sailboat approaches the shore.

Encourage your child to just breathe normally, paying attention to each individual breath and also to think how they are able to help the sailboat all the way back to shore; if they breathe too hard, they will blow the boat over and capsize it.

Keep encouraging your child to only pay attention to their breathing, and if they or you notice their attention wandering, which it will, e.g. thinking about their friend coming over to play later, ask them to refocus on their breathing.

(Your indicator that your child's attention is wondering is that their hands will stop coming together and will remain in the same position).

As your child continues to breathe, suggest to them that they may notice the movement in their upper body as they breathe, or they may feel a gentle tingle or tickle on their nostrils or lips.

The hack finishes when your child's hands come together to indicate that the sailboat is safely back to shore.

At the end of the hack, bring your child gently back into themselves asking them to open their eyes on the count of 5.

Again, like Hack 10, you might find that your child isn't able to stay focused for the whole hack the first few times. This is fine, just keep them going for as long as they remain interested.

HACK
12
NOTICING NATURE

Another great hack for getting your child to participate in mindfulness is by Noticing Nature. It will help your child to learn to be in the present moment whilst enjoying the pleasure of focusing on nature.

Mindfulness is all about being aware of the present moment and exploring it with all of your senses. Taking the opportunity to interact with nature can be a fantastic way to do this; it's very difficult for your child not to be amazed and excited by nature if they begin to really focus on it.

This hack requires you and your child to get out into nature; they will also get the benefits of being out in the fresh air and triggering some endorphins which are released with exercise.

Hack Time – 20 mins

What you will need – Being out in nature.

How it works

Take your child for a walk in nature. Ideally this would be in your local woods or beauty spot, but your garden can work equally well.

As you walk with your child, start by asking them to spend 5 minutes listening to the sounds of nature. The list below is a good way to try and identify the different sounds in nature:

- Can they hear 3 different bird songs and mimic them?
- Can they hear the wind blowing and rustling trees and bushes?
- Can they hear any insect or other animal sounds?

Then, whilst continuing your walk, ask your child to spend the next 5 minutes looking at the patterns in nature. The list below is useful for searching out the different patterns:

- Can they see 3 different types of patterns on different kinds of leaves?
- Can they see 3 different types of patterns on different types of tree bark?
- Can they see 3 different types of grass or moss?
- Can they see 3 different types of birds?
- Can they see 3 different types of animals?
- Can they see 3 different types of insects?

Then, as you walk, move onto exploring the smells in nature, ask your child to spend the next 5 minutes sniffing out the different smells in nature.

See if they can find 3 different flowers (be careful to avoid things like stinging nettles and brambles). Ask your child to try and describe the differences between the 3 different scents they discover.

For the final part of your Noticing Nature walk, ask your child to go back to the different kinds of leaves and bark they found earlier in the walk.

This time ask your child to feel the 3 different types of leaf and bark, ask them to describe how each one feels:

- Is it soft or hard?
- Is it rough or smooth?
- Is it slimy or dry?
- Is it flat or bobbly?

At the end of your walk, remind your child of all the different things that they have noticed in nature by hearing them, seeing them, touching them and smelling them. Ask your child to choose their favourite item from each category.

"Don't be a VICTIM of negative self-talk - remember YOU are listening."

Bob Proctor

CHAPTER 6
Self-talk and Questions

CHAPTER 6 – Self-talk and questions

It's often said that talking to yourself is the first sign of madness. Rest assured this is completely wrong; talking to yourself is actually a critical part of how we think. I would put self-talk down as one of the sure-fire indicators of sanity.

Whether it is just a dialogue you are having in your own head or a verbal dialogue you are having for all to hear, either way it's a positive thing. Your adherence to the restrictive nature of "social norms" will probably be the reason you don't talk aloud to yourself. Whereas your child is likely to feel a lot less inhibited about talking to themselves aloud, either way the key aspect is accepting that we do and we should talk to ourselves.

So, what is self-talk? It is something we all do naturally throughout our waking hours. It's the ongoing internal conversation we hold with ourselves and it has a very direct impact on our emotional response, such as our happiness and subsequent behaviours.

Let me give you an example, during the evening while I am watching TV on the sofa, I will notice that I'm starting to fall asleep. I may say to myself, "okay, time to head up to bed, I need to get up off the sofa before I fall fast asleep". Or alternatively, I may say, "it's so comfy here; I will spend just five more minutes enjoying this space". It is not possible for me to notice my circumstances and decide what to do, without having an internal dialogue. The only time I'm likely to respond to something without that internal dialogue is if I'm faced with a fight or flight situation and my primal instincts take over.

Self-talk is a way that you and your child articulate your thoughts to yourselves, and one of the key things we need to understand is that our thoughts are things; they have a life of their own. When it comes to interacting with the world around us, it's our thoughts that convey themselves to others through our vibrational energy and take precedence over the words we choose to say to the other parties.

Positive self-talk is something that you and your child can use to encourage yourselves to have good experiences and positive outcomes, because it provides an approach to stay motivated and remain confident.

Generally, people are becoming more aware of self-talk and realising that it provides us with a hugely powerful tool, if we can manage it and use it as a source of positivity for ourselves and others.

When it comes to your child, their self-talk is even more critical, it is likely they will face many more new experiences in any given week than an adult. Many of these new experiences can be very daunting, such as meeting new classmates, learning new topics or dealing with rejection in peer groups.

So, it's vital that parents are able to support and encourage their child to participate in positive self-talk. Because it will be the tone and content of your child's self-talk that will likely determine if your child has an enjoyable and successful experience or not.
If you teach your child about positive self-talk and support them in using it to build their confidence you can provide them with the ability to change a *"I can't do it"* to a more useful *"Yes, I can do it"*.

It's good for your child to understand that everybody has fears and doubts. The most important aspect is how they respond to them, so they don't just give into them without attempting to have an alternative perspective on the challenges they will inevitably face in the course of their young lives.

It is these alternative perspectives which will give them an opportunity to significantly influence the outcome of what it is they are about to do.

To master self-talk and use it as a force for good in your child's realisation of happiness, you need to help them do two things. Firstly, they need to be able to recognise when they are participating in negative self-talk. Most people are guilty of negative self-talk and we all need to stop doing it. Secondly, you also need to help and support your child in proactively introducing positive self-talk into their daily routine.

As **Bob Proctor**, the renowned mindset coach and contributor to *Rhonda Byrne's "The Secret"* film always says:

"Don't be a VICTIM of negative self-talk - remember YOU are listening."

For your child a typical sign that they are becoming a victim of their own negative self-talk is when they are finding something too difficult or if it's giving them a negative emotion or feelings of anxiety.

This is your opportunity to draw to your child's attention the fact they are having negative thoughts, which are being expressed in their self-talk.

Easy ways to recognise negative self-talk in your child is when you hear blanket generalisations and phrases such as:

- I can't
- I always
- I never
- I don't

Or if your child always expresses a negation such as:

- But
- Sometimes

This is when you can help your child by checking what is wrong or what is troubling them. Once you have understood the issue, then you can reassure them that everything is okay and offer up ways in which they can have a more positive perspective through the use of intentional and repetitive self-talk or by asking themselves a thought altering question.

In terms of the questions, anytime we ask ourselves a "why" question relating to a negative situation or belief, the answer we provide ourselves will only lead to a further re-enforcement of our current negative viewpoint. So, it's vital that you and your child are able to ask yourselves questions which will lead to an alternative, more open and encouraging perspective on the current challenge.

The hacks outlined in the rest of this chapter will give you some great ways to support your child in creating positive self-talk phrases and also how to ask themselves better positive thought-provoking questions.

HACK
13
I AM

This is a hack about intentionally generating positive self-talk phrases which you can use to help your child create and maintain a positive and open mindset. It also covers having any qualities they desire or current beliefs they are deficient in.

This hack is done by constructing a handful of specific phrases that represent the skills, qualities or abilities that your child wants to have. Following the instruction in this hack will trigger your child's unconscious mind to be supportive in the pursuit and belief that they already have the relevant items and qualities that they identify.

The trick with this hack is that it has to be performed on a regular and repetitive basis. Once the qualities have been identified, your child will repeat the same individual phrases each day until they believe they have achieved each desired quality.

Hack Time – 10 mins

What you will need – A sheet of paper or card, a pencil, blue tac or sticky tape.

How it works

Ask your child to think of a word that represents either a skill, ability or quality which they would like to fully believe they have for each of the following categories:

- A physical quality e.g. strong, tall, slim
- An emotional quality e.g. happy, joyful, curious
- A sporting quality e.g. fast, flexible, accurate
- A learning quality e.g. quick learner, good reader, neat writer
- A friendship quality e.g. kind, friendly, sharing
- A family quality e.g. loving, generous, caring

When your child has thought of their list of words which represent the various qualities, they desire for themselves, convert it into the following set of I AM phrases. The following is an example:

- I AM STRONG (physical quality)
- I AM CURIOUS (emotional quality)
- I AM ACCURATE (sporting quality)
- I AM A GOOD READER (learning quality)
- I AM KIND (friendship quality)
- I AM LOVING (family quality)

You could also add the following I AM phrases.

- I AM HAPPY
- I AM HEALTHY

Put all the above phrases onto a piece of paper or card and place it somewhere that your child will see on a regular basis, e.g. on their wardrobe door or bathroom mirror.

Then as part of a daily pattern encourage your child to repeat the phrases aloud 5 times in the morning and 5 times in the evening. One approach which we use, that works well, is to recite the I AM sayings on the commute to and from school.

The more emotion your child can express when saying it the more effective it will be.

HACK
14
HOW, WHAT AND
WHEN. NOT WHY.

This hack probably works better with older children, the purpose of it is to get your child to ask themselves better questions when participating in negative self-talk.

Often when your child is frustrated or disappointed about having not yet achieved something, their self-talk begins to head down the route of asking themselves "why".

For example, "**why** wasn't I asked to go to Jane's birthday party?".

When the questions relate to a negative thing, the answers that your self-talk provides will only continue to re-enforce the negative feeling. If you are asking "why" I didn't achieve X, the answers can't be positive, because you are exploring why something hasn't happened.

Therefore, it's vital that you find another line of questioning, which will ensure a more positive and optimistic mindset can be maintained.

Hack Time – 5 mins

What you will need – A sheet of paper, a pencil.

How it works

This is what we call a trigger hack, e.g. you only need to do it when you have heard your child express certain language.

So, whenever you hear your child say something like:

- I'm disappointed about
- I'm sad because
- Why can't I
- Why don't I

Then you should ask them to participate in the following hack.

First determine what it is that your child is sad, upset or disappointed about. Once you have established this, e.g. they are upset that they didn't have a friend to play with at lunchtime.

Then ask your child to answer the following questions.

- **How** could I get a friend to play with at lunchtime?
- **When** will I ask Johnny to play with me at lunchtime?
- **What** do I need to do differently to have a friend to play with at lunchtime?

Capture your child's answers and then read them back to your child.

The final step is to ask your child to say, based on the answers that they have given, what two things will they do differently tomorrow.

This hack is very effective because by getting your child to ask themselves How, What and When questions they will then be seeking positive solutions to their issue rather then re-enforcing their negative view.

It may also be that whatever your child's issue is, it can also be turned into a positive statement as part of the Daily Sayings in Hack 17.

HACK
15
BEST AND BETTER

Most negative self-talk begins as your child spends time thinking about things which they aren't good or successful at.

It is very easy to get caught up focussing on all the things we aren't good at and spend very little time reflecting on and celebrating what we are good at. The benefits of your child seeing themselves in a positive light are massive and infectious; it will start to build a positive self-image for your child, and self-image is something that you can never outperform. The more activities and hacks you can do to build your child's self-image, the better.

Hack Time – 10 mins

What you will need – A sheet of paper, a pencil.

How it works

Ask your child to make a list of 10 things which they feel they are BEST at.

When your child has finished the list, get them to rank the list of 10 things they are best at and write down one reason why they find it easy to be best at that activity.

Your child's best list will probably look something like the example below.

Best at list….

a) Getting ready for school on time   **Rank** 3

   Reason – I keep an eye on the time

b) Scoring penalties in football   **Rank** 1

Reason – I can kick the ball very hard

c) Making people laugh   **Rank** 2

Reason – Because I read and remember a lot of jokes

Then ask your child to make a list of 10 things which they are getting better at.

Make sure your child understands that the key thing about the term **getting better** is that it's something they are improving at, irrespective of the start point and where they currently are. For example, not knowing the entire alphabet, but only knowing the vowels, is still an improvement when compared to not knowing any of the alphabet.

Once they have created their list of things, which they are getting better at, ask your child to then write down one reason why they think they are getting better at it.

Better at list……..

a) Tying my shoelaces

Reason – I keep practising

b) Cleaning out my hamster

Reason – I have put it on my calendar to do every Sunday

c) Asking for help in class

Reason – Because I know my teachers want to help me.

The significance of the getting better list is, it helps your child see something which they may have been struggling with in a more positive light; they are focusing on the improvement, rather than the fact they can't do it yet.

Also, the identification of the reason why they are best at something or getting better, is because these reasons can potentially be applied to other situations and circumstances where your child may be using negative self-talk.

HACK
16
SELF-TALK BINGO

This hack is all about helping your child become self-aware of when they are participating in both positive and negative self-talk.

Becoming more self-aware of self-talk will in turn enable your child to have more conscious control about when to trigger positive self-talk in situations and circumstances which they are finding difficult.

Hack Time – All day

What you will need – A sheet of paper, a pencil.

How it works

Create a list of negative self-talk terms and phrases which your child may say and write them on a piece of paper in a grid.

Also, on the grid have a number of columns marked up "when", it should look like the example below.

	When	**When**	**When**	**When**
I'm not good at this				
I can't do it				
I know I won't do it				
It never goes right				

I've ruined it				
I'm worried about				
I'm scared				
I hate doing this				

Give the grid to your child and ask them to notice each time they are saying any of the phrases in the grid. This can be either when they are saying the phrase aloud or just internally in their head.

Once your child notices that they have said one of the phrases, ask them to notice and write down when it happened e.g. it happened when I was trying to finish my homework.

At the end of the day review the list with your child. For each occasion they have identified the use of a negative self-talk phrase work together on what could have been an alternative more beneficial positive self-talk phrase.

"You can steer yourself in any direction you choose."

Dr Seuss

CHAPTER 7
Goals and Intentions

CHAPTER 7 – Goals and Intentions

When we think of goals, typically we would think of them as something reserved for adults; it is however also very important that you start to setup the notion of both goals and intentions with your child.

When we think about realising happiness, this is usually accomplished by focusing on the following three areas:

- Being reconciled with the **past**
- Being focused and fully engaged with the **now**
- Having goals in the **future** that motivate and inspire you

Let me begin by identifying the differences between a goal and an intention.

A goal is focused on a future achievement or outcome which will have a timeframe relating to it. Typically, a goal will relate to some type of externally identifiable success, e.g. learning to read to a certain standard or being given a part in the next school play.

Whereas, an intention relates to the present moment and is typically a way of being or thinking; it doesn't necessarily have a specific externally recognisable outcome. Intentions are about how you or your child wants to be within themselves.

Being aware of and consciously focusing on goals and intentions will help support your child with both the now and the future elements of the equation.

It will enable your child to feel in control of their life from a young age. It encourages them towards being at cause for what happens to them rather than being at effect.   Contrary to what some parents want their children to believe, your child is able to make choices about many aspects of their lives.

This sentiment is nicely captured in the phrase used by **Dr Seuss**, the American author, animator and film maker:

"You can steer yourself in any direction you choose."

Understanding goals and intentions also reinforces a positive mindset. It encourages your child to be aware of the huge amount of potential which can be tapped into and fulfilled through the pursuit of goals which they are genuinely interested in and motivated by.

It will also provide your child will an opportunity for mindful reflection. They can begin to think about themselves, their lives and who, how and what they want to be. This is particularly pertinent if the parent doesn't try and influence what goals and intentions their child wants to set.

It's more likely your child will excel and enthuse in pursuit of a self-generated goal, whereas they may well resist and procrastinate if a goal is being pushed upon them. Being a dutiful and complicit child, doesn't necessarily make for a happy child.

As a parent, you can really start to support and help your child with the setting of goals and intentions by trying to influence their structure and format, rather than the actual idea itself.

It would be good for your child to have a balanced set of intentions and goals, for example, one relating to school, one relating to their favourite hobby and one related to how they generally want to conduct themselves.

In addition, to help your child build, and maintain confidence, without stifling their raw ambition. You may want to help your child formulate incremental goals which are aligned to their overall goal.

For example, if your child has a goal of becoming an astronaut, to you this may seem like a very difficult goal to achieve and certainly one which can't be accomplished until much later in life. In order to support them on this goal suggest that they introduce some other goals along the way, which will be aligned with their ultimate goal of being an astronaut.

You could suggest that their first mini goal is to join the local Air Cadets. Then further   goals of getting qualifications in relevant topics, like physics, maths and chemistry.

This will help your child to understand the importance and benefits of maintaining long-term motivation and perseverance, rather than giving up because the goal seems unobtainable and feeling like they have failed.

Your child will go through a huge amount of change and development throughout their childhood. As they learn new things about themselves and the wider world, don't be surprised if this evolution is reflected in a desire to continually tweak or change their stated goals and intentions.

It's much better that your child has a notion of goals and intentions and how they have the power of choice to shape their life to be happy and fulfilled, than it is to make sure a stated goal is completed if it no longer resonates with your child.

HACK
17
DAILY SAYING

This hack is very similar to Hack 15 in the Self-talk and Questions section. However, this time you are looking to generate a positive statement to help your child create and maintain a positive and open mindset to achieving a particular goal which your child most desires.

This hack is achieved by constructing a specific short saying which will trigger their unconscious minds to be supportive in the pursuit of what they want

The trick with this hack is that it has to be done on a regular and repetitive basis. Once the saying is created your child will then repeat the same saying till they have achieved that stated desire.

Hack Time – 10 mins

What you will need – A sheet of paper or card, a pencil, blue tac or sticky tape.

How it works

Ask your child to tell you which achievement they currently most desire. This could be something like "getting their school pen license" or "becoming a free reader" or "getting a place in the school football team".

Once they have shared their desire with you, you then need to complete the following template with them to construct their daily saying. It's important that you follow the format exactly; it has been constructed in a way which will maximise the impact of your child's self-talk.

Daily Saying template:

I am so ....

Ask your child to select a positive emotion which they will feel when they have successfully achieved their desire e.g. happy, excited, thrilled, proud, joyful **and grateful.**

Now that I am ....

Fill in your child's stated achievement e.g. I am passing all my maths tests.

Give as much detail as possible and make sure this statement is expressed in the positive, as your child's unconscious mind can't process a negative, e.g. don't say now that I have stopped failing my maths test.

The final completed saying would look something like this:

I am so proud and grateful that I have successfully passed my end of term maths test.

Once the daily saying has been created with your child, put it on a piece of paper or card and place it somewhere your child will see it on a regular basis e.g. on their wardrobe door or bathroom mirror.

As part of a daily pattern encourage your child to repeat the saying aloud 5 times in the morning and 5 times in the evening. One approach which works well is to recite the daily saying on the commute to and from school.

The more emotion your child can express when saying it the more effective it will be.

HACK
18
VISION BOARD

This is a great hack for any children who enjoy arts and crafts, it will get them engaged with one of their favourite activities. A vision board is a great way to help your child literally visualise their goals.

The creation of a vision board is a great way for your child to be mindful and spend time focusing on the things which they do want; if your child doesn't put any thought into how they want their future to be, they can find themselves driven and responding to external events and other peoples wishes.

By using a vision board, you are asking your child to identify and find images that represent all of the things which they would like to possess or experience in their lives. The vision board can then act as a magnet and reminder for your child's unconscious mind, helping them to make choices which will lead them in the direction of the items on the vision board.

Hack Time – 30 mins

What you will need – A sheet of card, colouring pencils, glue, kid friendly scissors, old magazines, a PC or tablet and a printer.

How it works

Ask your child to come and sit with you at a table.

Give them a stack of old magazines and ask them to flick through and cut out any images which represent things they would like to have, possess or experience. It's like creating a shopping list for life.

Encourage your child to only select the things which they desire for themselves. It won't be as effective if they are selecting things which they believe other people want.

When your child has finished cutting out all of the images they are interested in, ask them to choose 6 to 10 of their favourite images which depict different things.

For each of their favourite images, ask them if this image is exactly what they desire, or would they like to look on the internet for an even more specific image. Just like Hack 17, it's good for your child to be as detailed and specific as possible.

If your child wants an even more specific image of what they desire, then sit with them and search google images for a better fit.

When your child finds their preferred image print it out and add it to their favourite image pile.

When all the favourite images have been assembled, they can then begin sticking them on to the piece of card in any order and design that they like best.

Your child can also add any additional decorations to their vision board which helps bring it to life and make it even more eye catching for them. This can include adding words or phrases which have meaning to them.

When the vision board is fully decorated, find a place somewhere in your house to hang it where your child will frequently see it.

The creation of the vision board is a fabulous and fun way for your child to set their intentions for what they would like. It's also something you can do for yourself at the same time as your child.

HACK
19
INTENTION QUESTIONS

This hack is a very good informal way of getting your child to think and articulate what their intentions for the day are.

It works particularly well because your child doesn't need to have an understanding of what an intention is, they are just answering questions, which will then put their intentions at the forefront of their mind.

At the end of the day, there is no need to check or validate if your child has achieved their stated intentions. The purpose of this hack is to help your child realise that they can take control of their desires and actions.

It will be easier for your child to realise their happiness, and have a sense of purpose and wellbeing, if they are able to strive for the things which they have a desire and interest in.

Hack Time – 10 mins

What you will need – N/A

How it works

Start a conversation with your child whilst you are engaged in some type of activity at the start of the day, e.g. getting dressed, having breakfast or driving to school.

During that conversation ask your child some, or all, of the following questions listed below, you may need to adapt or amend this list based on your child's age:

- How do you want to feel today?
- What do you want to achieve today?
- What would make you proud today?
- How do you want to play or engage with others today?

- Who are you going to be kind to today?
- Who are you going to help today?
- What's the most important thing to you today?
- Is there something bothering you that you would like to talk about today?
- What are you most excited about today?
- What are you most grateful for today?
- What will make you very happy today?

As your child answers each question, help to re-enforce their intentions by saying something positive about it. For example:

- That's a great thing to be grateful for.
- It will be so wonderful when you achieve that.
- That makes me happy too.
- I'm sure they will be very grateful for your help.
- That would make me very proud of you too.

In addition, you could also answer the same questions for yourself and share the answers with your child, because this is another good way to demonstrate that you set intentions for the day too.

HACK
20
SMART GOALS

I'm sure you have already heard of SMART goals. It's a concept created by **George T. Doran**, a consultant and former Director of Corporate Planning for Washington Water Power back in 1981. The concept is to ensure that your goal contains the following attributes:

- Specific
- Measurable
- Achievable
- Relevant
- Timed

This concept has been widely adopted by business and personal coaches; the reason being, it really does help people apply the right levels of definition and commitment to their chosen goal. Because setting and achieving goals leads to a sense of fulfilment and purpose, it can have a direct impact on your happiness.

Based on the above we see SMART goals as being a hack that can also work well with your child, particularly if they are aged 10 and above.

Hack Time – 20 mins

What you will need – A sheet of paper, a pencil.

How it works

Ask your child to identify the goal which they are most excited and motivated to achieve. Once again confirm this is a goal that they want to achieve for themselves, and not for someone else.

Then take them through the following questions to help define and refine their chosen goal.

Firstly, ask your child to be very **specific** about the goal they want to achieve. For example, if your child's goal is to do better at school, you need to encourage them to put this into very specific language, like; I want to get better grades in Maths, English and Drama.

Then to make it **measurable,** ask your child to say how they will know that they have achieved their goal. If they can't measure that they have been successful, then it will be impossible to say the goal has been achieved. Using the example above, your child will need to further refine their goal to be something like; I want to get a 10% improvement in my end of year grades for Maths, English and Drama compared to last year.

Then validate with your child that they see this goal as being **achievable**. This is important, if your child doesn't see their goal as achievable, then it will not be something that motivates their efforts in striving for their goal.

If they say they don't think their goal is achievable then ask them to refine the goal to something which is achievable, for example, they may want to reduce the goal to be a 5% improvement.

At this point you also need to check with your child that their stated goal is **relevant**. There are two aspects to this, firstly, is their chosen goal worthwhile to them. The best way to establish this is to ask your child why they want to achieve this goal, a very big why will give them a lot of emotional energy to drive their actions.

Secondly, is it something that is important to your child right now? For example, they might want to get better grades by the end of the year, however there could be something more pressing. For example, they may have the lead part in the school play and need to learn hundreds of lines in the next month. Let your child decide if their goal is relevant to them; you can guide them by offering alternative goals which they can either accept or reject.

Finally, you need to ask your child to put a **timeframe** on when they want to achieve the goal by. In the example we are using, there is already a timeframe set with the goal happening at the end of the school year.

But if no timeframe is associated with the goal ask your child to define a timeframe, for younger children you may want to encourage a shorter timeframe as their attention span is likely to be shorter.

Once you have asked your child all of the questions above, then ask them to write down their goal on a piece of paper. There is a lot of documented research showing that goals which are written down have a much greater chance of being achieved.

In our experience, we often find that the biggest challenge children have with achieving their goals is the goals are either too big or too hard to achieve. Using the SMART goals hack will greatly assist with overcoming this issue.

"In all this world there is nothing so beautiful as a happy child."

L. Frank Baum

Epilogue

We are hopeful that you will not have found any of the content of this book too difficult or too daunting to do with your child.

The premise of the book is to provide parents, teachers and carers with a toolkit of different activities and exercises which can be undertaken with your child on a regular basis to support and develop your child's ability to realise, maintain and cultivate their feelings of happiness.

We have attempted to share with you the knowledge we have acquired over the last 20 years together with the exercises and activities we have applied to our own children. Over the last 5 years we have undertaken a lot of practical research and made refinements to some of the hacks based on our own trial and error experiences with our own children.

On the assumption your child is anything like ours, they won't always be in the right mood or frame of mind to actively and willingly participate in these types of activities. We would therefore always advocate that the emphasis should be on enjoyment and fun. All learning is unconscious; your child will get very little from any of these hacks if they are forced to participate, with the exception of the ones in the physiology section, which will have an immediate impact.

Your child's happiness will illuminate their life, but it will also begin to illuminate your life too. As **L. Frank Baum** the author of *The Wizard of Oz* says:

"In all this world there is nothing so beautiful as a happy child."

But we do have to bear in mind that we cannot be responsible for our child's happiness. Everyone is responsible for their own happiness; as parents, what we are responsible for is being a good happiness role model and teaching our children the importance of happiness and the key components for being happy. This is where the hacks in this book become invaluable.

Even the most perfect parent, if there is such a thing, cannot make their child realise happiness. So please don't try to chase perfection, you won't achieve it and the pursuit of perfection is likely to lead you to be miserable, which will be of no use to you or your child.

Our recommendation is to take the hacks outlined in this book and utilise on a regular basis the ones which your child enjoys the most. We most definitely wouldn't suggest that you try and do all of the exercises every week, you are not looking to take your children through a happiness regime. What you are looking to do is introduce and re-enforce a positive and optimistic mindset in your child towards realising and maintaining happiness.

We would love to hear your feedback regarding which hacks your child has enjoyed and benefited from. Equally we would welcome your feedback on any hacks which you found difficult or your child hasn't enjoyed.

We would also be very interested in hearing about any other hacks, activities and exercises which you have successfully used with your child. We are constantly looking to learn and expand our knowledge concerning how we can support children in realising their happiness.

Perhaps your hack could be included in a *Happy Hacks for Kids Volume 2*.

Wishing both you and your child much happiness.

Richard & Lisa

Visit our websites

www.happinessacademy.online

and

www.polaritypublishing.co.uk

for more information about our trainings, workshops and other books.

Plus, lots of FREE resources.

About the Authors

Richard and Lisa met in 2006 whilst working together on a change initiative for a major FTSE100 company. They had a shared interest in understanding the principles of change and the psychology that underpins successful change in both individuals and organisations.

By 2009 they were married and started their own consultancy, Transformation Station Ltd, which specialises in Change and Transformation for individuals and organisations.

Over the years they have worked with many blue-chip clients, local authorities and government departments. However, the work they do with individuals is what they find most rewarding; successful change in an individual can have a very profound and transformational impact on the individual's life.

Although both Richard and Lisa achieved very few qualifications whilst at school, they both developed a passion for learning during adulthood and now have a string of academic, professional and therapeutic qualifications between them. They view this desire to continually learn, grow and develop to be one of the cornerstones of both their marriage and business partnership.

Richard is a mindset expert, specialising in a combination of Happiness and Personal Goal Achievement. He is the author of the bestselling book "*Happiness Realised – The inside guide to achieving lasting happiness*" and the creator of "*R.A.D.A.R the Goal Achievement System*". His work has been featured on BBC Radio Kent and BBC 3 Counties Radio.

Lisa is a transformational change expert working with both executive teams to implement large scale organisational change and with individuals wanting to achieve a personal breakthrough. Lisa is privileged to have had the opportunity to work with 1000's of veterans and serving personnel through her activities with The Warrior Programme charity.

Richard and Lisa have a total of 4 children covering an 18-year age span. The eldest two children are from Richard's first marriage to Nicola and the youngest two children are from Richard and Lisa's marriage, despite being told by their doctor that they only had a 1% chance of having children together.

Richard and Lisa have a very progressive view on parenting and firmly believe in children having the opportunity to both think for themselves and have platforms to express themselves. They both advocate the importance of teaching your child how to think, and not what to think.

Most children are naturally happy, and it is only their external influences which will start to undermine their natural happiness. This is why they are such big advocates in using proactive activities and exercises as the best methods for helping children to maintain their happiness and reduce the risk of children developing mental health challenges in later life.

Printed in Great Britain
by Amazon